THE FOUNDATIONS OF MINDFULNESS
Satipaṭṭhāna Sutta

Translated by
Nyanasatta Thera

Buddhist Publication Society
P.O. Box 61,
54, Sangharaja Mawatha,
Kandy, Sri Lanka.

First published: 1960
Reprints: 1968, 1974, 1982, 1993, 2000, 2012

Copyright (©) by Buddhist Publication Society

National Library and Documentation Services Board -
Cataloguing-In-Publication Data

Nyanasatta Himi,
  The Foundations of Mindfulness: Satipaṭṭhāna
  Sutta /Nyanasatta Himi.- Kandy: Buddhist
  Publication Society Inc., 2012
  BP 522.- 34p.; 18.5cm.

  ISBN 978-955-24-0384-2

  i. 294.3823 DDC 23   ii. Title
  1. Suttapitaka

ISBN: 978-955-24-0384-2

Printed by
Ruchira Printers
Kandy—Sri Lanka

INTRODUCTION

The Philosophy of Buddhism is contained in the Four Noble Truths

The *truth of suffering*[1] reveals that all forms of becoming, all the various elements of existence comprised in the "five aggregates" or groups of existence—also called the "five categories which are the objects of clinging" *(pañcupadānakkhandhā)*—are inseparable from suffering as long as they remain objects of grasping or clinging. All corporeality, all feelings and sensations, all perceptions, all mental formations and consciousness, being impermanent, are a source of suffering, are conditioned phenomena and hence not-self *(anicca, dukkha, anattā)*. Ceaseless origination and dissolution best characterize the process of existence called life, for all elements of this flux of becoming continually arise from conditions created by us and then pass away, giving rise to new elements of being according to one's actions or kamma.

All suffering originates from craving, and our very existence is conditioned by craving, which is threefold: the craving for sense pleasures *(kāma-taṇhā)*, craving for continued and renewed existence *(bhava-taṇhā)*, and

---

1. An exhaustive exposition of the Four Noble Truths is found in *The Word of the Buddha* by Nyanatiloka Mahāthera. See also *Three Cardinal Discourses of the Buddha*, translated by Ñāṇamoli Thera (BPS Wheel No. 17) and *The Four Noble Truths* by Francis Story (BPS Wheel No. 34/35).

craving for annihilation after death *(vibhava-taṇhā)*. This is the *truth of the origin of suffering.*

The attainment of perfect happiness, the breaking of the chain of rebirths and suffering through the realization of Nibbāna, is possible only through the utter extirpation of that threefold craving. This is the *truth of suffering's cessation.*

The methods of training for the liberation from all suffering are applied by following the Noble Eightfold Path of Right Understanding, Right Thought, Right Speech, Right Action, Right Living, Right Exertion, Right Mindfulness and Right Concentration of Mind. The Noble Eightfold Path consists of three types of training summed up in: virtuous conduct *(sīla)*, concentration *(samādhi)* and wisdom *(paññā)*. This is the *truth of the way that leads to the cessation of suffering.*

The prevalence of suffering and absence of freedom and happiness is due to man's subjection to the three roots of all unskill and evil, and all unwholesome actions *(akusalakamma)*, viz. lust, hatred and delusion *(lobha, dosa, moha)*.

Virtuous conduct casts out lust. The calm of true concentration and mental culture conquers hatred. Wisdom or right understanding, also called direct knowledge resulting from meditation, dispels all delusion. All these three types of training are possible only through the cultivation of constant *mindfulness (sati)*, which forms the seventh link of the Noble Eightfold Path. Mindfulness is called a controlling faculty *(indriya)* and a spiritual power *(bala)*, and is also the first of the seven factors of enlightenment *(satta bojjhaṅga)*.[2] Right Mindfulness *(samma-sati)* has to be present in every skillful or karmically

---

2. See Piyadassi Thera, *The Seven Factors of Enlightenment* (BPS Wheel No. 1).

wholesome thought moment *(kusalacitta)*. It is the basis of all earnest endeavour *(appamāda)* for liberation, and maintains in us the sense of urgency to strive for enlightenment or Nibbāna.

The Discourse on the Foundations of Mindfulness, the *Satipaṭṭhāna Sutta,* is the tenth discourse of the Middle Length Collection (Majjhima Nikāya) of the Discourses of the Enlightened One. It is this version which is translated in the present publication. There is another version of it, in the Collection of Long Discourses (Dīgha Nikāya No. 22), which differs only by a detailed explanation of the Four Noble Truths.

The great importance of the Discourse on Mindfulness has never been lost to the Buddhists of the Theravada tradition. In Sri Lanka, even when the knowledge and practice of the Dhamma was at its lowest ebb through centuries of foreign domination, the Sinhala Buddhists never forgot the Satipaṭṭhāna Sutta. Memorizing the Sutta has been an unfailing practice among the Buddhists, and even today in Sri Lanka there are large numbers who can recite the Sutta from memory. It is a common sight to see on full-moon days devotees who are observing the Eight Precepts, engaged in community recital of the Sutta. Buddhists are intent on hearing this Discourse even in the last moments of their lives; and at the bedside of a dying Buddhist either monks or laymen recite this venerated text.

In the private shrine room of a Buddhist home, the book of the Satipaṭṭhāna Sutta is displayed prominently as an object of reverence. Monastery libraries of palm-leaf manuscripts have the Sutta bound in highly ornamented covers.

One such book with this Discourse written in Sinhala script on palm-leaf, has found its way from Sri Lanka as far as the State University Library of Bucharest in Rumania. This was disclosed while collecting material for the Encyclopaedia of Buddhism, when an Esperantist correspondent gave us a list of a hundred books on Buddhism found in the Rumanian University Libraries.

Mindfulness of Breathing (*Ānāpānasati*)

The subjects dealt with in the Satipaṭṭhāna Sutta are corporeality, feeling, mind and mind objects, being the universe of right Buddhist contemplation for deliverance. A very prominent place in the Discourse is occupied by the discussion on mindfulness of breathing *(ānāpānasati)*. To make the present publication of greater practical value to the reader, an introductory exposition of the methods of practicing that particular meditation will now be given.

Mindfulness of breathing takes the highest place among the various subjects of Buddhist meditation. It has been recommended and praised by the Enlightened One thus: "This concentration through mindfulness of breathing, when developed and practiced much, is both peaceful and sublime, it is an unadulterated blissful abiding, and it banishes at once and stills evil unprofitable thoughts as soon as they arise." Though of such a high order, the initial stages of this meditation are well within the reach of a beginner though he be only a lay student of the Buddha-Dhamma. Both in the Discourse here translated, and in the 118th Discourse of the same Collection (the Majjhima Nikāya), which specifically deals with that meditation, the initial instructions for the practice are clearly laid down:

Herein, monks, a monk, having gone to the forest or the root of a tree or to an empty place, sits down with his legs crossed, keeps his body erect and his mindfulness alert. Ever mindful he breathes in, mindful he breathes out. Breathing in a long breath, he knows, "I am breathing in a long breath"; breathing out a long breath, he knows, "I am breathing out a long breath." Breathing in a short breath, he knows, "I am breathing in a short breath"; breathing out a short breath, he knows, "I am breathing out a short breath." "Experiencing the whole (breath) body, I shall breathe in," thus he trains himself. "Experiencing the whole (breath-) body, I shall breathe out," thus he trains himself. "Calming the activity of the (breath-) body, I shall breathe in," thus he trains himself. "Calming the activity of the (breath-) body, I shall breathe out," thus he trains himself.

These are instructions given by the Enlightened One to the monks who, after their alms round, had the whole remaining day free for meditation. But what about the lay Buddhist who has a limited time to devote to this practice? Among the places described as fit for the practice of meditation, one is available to all: *suññagara*, lit. "empty house," may mean any room in the house that has no occupant at that moment, and one may in the course of the twenty-four hours of the day find a room in one's house that is empty and undisturbed. Those who work all day and feel too tired in the evening for meditation may devote the early hours of the morning to the practice of mindfulness of breathing.

The other problem is the right posture for meditation. The full "lotus posture" of the yogi, the *padmasana*, as we see it in the Buddha statues, proves nowadays rather difficult to many, even to easterners. A youthful meditator, however, or even a middle-aged one, can well train himself in that posture in stages. He may, for instance, start with sitting on a low, broad chair or bed, bending only one leg and resting the other on the floor; and so, in gradual approximation, he may finally master that posture. There are also other easier postures of sitting with legs bent, for instance the half-lotus posture. It will be worth one's effort to train oneself in such postures; but if one finds them difficult and uncomfortable at the outset it will not be advisable to delay or disturb one's start with meditation proper on that account. One may allow a special time for sitting-practice, using it as best as one can for contemplation and reflection; but for the time being, the practice of meditation aiming at higher degrees of concentration may better be done in a posture that is comfortable. One may sit on a straight backed chair of a height that allows the legs to rest comfortably on the floor without strain. As soon however, as a cross-legged posture has become more comfortable, one should assume it for the practice of mindfulness of breathing, since it will allow one to sit in meditation for a longer time than is possible on a chair.

The meditator's body and mind should be alert but not tense. A place with a dimmed light will be profitable since it will help to exclude diverting attention to visible objects.

The right place, time and posture are very important and often essential for a successful meditative effort.

Though we have been breathing throughout our life, we have done so devoid of mindfulness, and hence, when we try to follow each breath attentively, we find that the Buddhist teachers of old were right when they compared the natural state of an uncontrolled mind to an untamed calf. Our minds have long been dissipated among visible data and other objects of the senses and of thought, and hence do not yield easily to attempts at mind-control.

Suppose a cowherd wanted to tame a wild calf: he would take it away from the cow and tie it up apart with a rope to a stout post. Then the calf might dash to and fro, but being unable to get away and tired after its effort, it would eventually lie down by the post. So too, when the meditator wants to tame his own mind that has long been reared on the enjoyment of sense objects, he should take it away from places where these sense objects abound, and tie the mind to the post of in-breaths and out-breaths with the rope of mindfulness. And though his mind may then dash to and fro when deprived of its liberty to roam among the sense objects, it will ultimately settle down when mindfulness is persistent and strong.

When practicing mindfulness of breathing, attention should be focused at the tip of the nose or at the point of the upper lip immediately below where the current of air can be felt. The meditator's attention should not leave this "focusing point" from where the in-coming and out-going breaths can be easily felt and observed. The meditator may become aware of the breath's route through the body but he should not pay attention to it. At the beginning of the practice, the meditator should concentrate only on the in-breaths and out-breaths, and should not fall into any reflections about them. It is only at a later stage that he should apply himself to the arousing of knowledge and other states connected with the concentration.

In this brief introduction, only the first steps of the beginner can be discussed. For more information the student may refer to the English translation of the *Visuddhimagga (The Path of Purification,* chap. VIII) by Bhikkhu Ñāṇamoli, or to *Mindfulness of Breathing* by Bhikkhu Ñāṇamoli, and to *The Heart of Buddhist Meditation* by Nyanaponika Thera.[3]

The lay Buddhist who undertakes this practice will first take the Three Refuges and the Five Precepts; he will review the reflections on the Buddha, Dhamma, and Sangha, transmit thoughts of loving-kindness *(mettā)* in all directions, recollect that this meditation will help him to reach the goal of deliverance through direct knowledge and

---

3. All published by the Buddhist Publication Society.

mental calm; and only then should he start with the mindfulness of breathing proper, first by way of counting.[4]

Counting

The Buddhist teachers of old recommend that a beginner should start the practice by counting the breaths mentally. In doing so he should not stop short of five or go beyond ten or make any break in the series. By stopping short of five breaths his mind has not enough room for contemplation, and by going beyond ten his mind takes the number rather than the breaths for its objects, and any break in the series would upset the meditation.

When counting, the meditator should first count when the in-breath or the out-breath is completed, not when it begins. So taking the in-breath first, he counts mentally 'one' when that in-breath is complete, then he counts 'two' when the out-breath is complete, 'three' after the next in-breath, and so on up to ten, and then again from one to ten, and so he should continue.

After some practice in counting at the completion of a breath, breathing may becoming faster. The breaths, however, should not be made longer or shorter intentionally. The meditator has to be just mindful of their occurrence as they come and go. Now he may try counting 'one' when he *begins* to breathe in or breathe out, counting up to five or ten, and then again from one to five or ten. If one takes both the in-breath and out-breath as 'one,' it is better to count only up to five.

Counting should be employed until one can dispense with it in following the sequence of breaths successively. Counting is merely a device to assist in

---

4. On the Refuges and Precepts, see *The Mirror of the Dhamma* (BPS Wheel No. 54).

excluding stray thoughts. It is, as it were, a guideline or railing for supporting mindfulness until it can do without such help. There may be those who will feel the counting more as a complication than a help, and they may well omit it, attending directly to the flow of the respiration by way of "connecting the successive breaths."

Connecting

After the counting has been discarded, the meditator should now continue his practice by way of connecting *(anubandhana)*; that is, by following mindfully the in and out breaths without recourse to counting, and yet without a break in attentiveness. Here too, the breaths should not be followed beyond the nostrils where the respiratory air enters and leaves. The meditator must strive to be aware of the whole breath, in its entire duration and without missing one single phase, but his attention must not leave the place of contact, the nostrils, or that point of the upper lip where the current of air touches.

While following the in-breaths and out-breaths thus, they become fainter and fainter, and at times it is not easy to remain aware of that subtle sensation of touch caused by the respiration. Keener mindfulness is required to keep track of the breaths then. But if the meditator perseveres, one day he will feel a different sensation, a feeling of ease and happiness, and occasionally there appears before his mental eye something like a luminous star or a similar sign, which indicates that one approaches the stage of access concentration. Steadying the newly acquired sign, one may cultivate full mental absorption *(jhāna)* or at least the preliminary concentration as a basis for practicing insight.

The practice of mindfulness of breathing is meant for both mental calm and insight *(samatha* and *vipassanā)*.

Direct knowledge being the object of Buddhist meditation, the concentration gained by the meditative practice should be used for the clear understanding of reality as manifest in oneself and in the entire range of one's experience.

Though penetrative insight leading to Nibbāna is the ultimate object, progress in mindfulness and concentration will also bring many benefits in our daily lives. If we have become habituated to follow our breaths for a longer period of time and can exclude all (or almost all) intruding irrelevant thoughts, mindfulness, self-control and efficiency are sure to increase in all our activities. Just as our breathing, so also other processes of body and mind, will become clearer to us, and we shall come to know more of ourselves.

It has been said by the Buddha: "Mindfulness of breathing, developed and repeatedly practiced, is of great fruit, of great advantage, for it fulfils the four foundations of mindfulness; the four foundations of mindfulness, developed and repeatedly practiced, fulfil the seven enlightenment factors; the seven enlightenment factors, developed and repeatedly practiced, fulfil clear-vision and deliverance." Clear vision and deliverance, or direct knowledge and the bliss of liberation, are the highest fruit of the application of mindfulness.

THE FOUNDATIONS OF MINDFULNESS
Satipaṭṭhāna Sutta

Thus have I heard. At one time the Blessed One was living among the Kurus, at Kammāsadamma, a market town of the Kuru people. There the Blessed One addressed the bhikkhu thus: "Monks," and they replied to him, "Venerable Sir." The Blessed One spoke as follows:

This is the only way, monks, for the purification of beings, for the overcoming of sorrow and lamentation, for the destruction of suffering and grief, for reaching the right path, for the attainment of Nibbāna, namely, the four foundations of mindfulness. What are the four?

Herein (in this teaching) a monk lives contemplating the body in the body,[5] ardent, clearly comprehending and mindful, having overcome, in this world, covetousness and grief; he lives contemplating feelings in feelings,

---

5. The repetition of the phrases 'contemplating the body in the body,' 'feelings in feelings,' etc. is meant to impress upon the meditator the importance of remaining aware whether, in the sustained attention directed upon a single chosen object, one is still keeping to it, and has not strayed into the field of another contemplation. For instance, when contemplating any bodily process, a meditator may unwittingly be side-tracked into a consideration of his *feelings* connected with that bodily process. He should then be clearly aware that he has left his original subject, and is engaged in the contemplation of feeling.

ardent, clearly comprehending and mindful, having overcome, in this world, covetousness and grief; he lives contemplating consciousness in consciousness,[6] ardent, clearly comprehending and mindful, having overcome, in this world, covetousness and grief; he lives contemplating mental objects in mental objects, ardent, clearly comprehending and mindful, having overcome, in this world, covetousness and grief.

I. THE CONTEMPLATION OF THE BODY
1. Mindfulness of Breathing

And how does a monk live contemplating the body in the body?

Herein, monks, a monk, having gone to the forest, to the foot of a tree or to an empty place, sits down with his legs crossed, keeps his body erect and his mindfulness alert.[7]

Ever mindful he breathes in, mindful he breathes out. Breathing in a long breath, he knows, "I am breathing in a long breath"; breathing out a long breath, he knows, "I am breathing out a long breath"; breathing in a short breath, he knows, "I am breathing in a short breath"; breathing out a short breath, he knows, "I am breathing out a short breath."

"Experiencing the whole (breath-) body, I shall breathe in," thus he trains himself. "Experiencing the whole (breath-) body, I shall breathe out," thus he trains

---

6. Mind (Pali *citta*, also consciousness or *viññāṇa*) in this connection means the states of mind or units in the stream of mind of momentary duration. Mental objects, *dhamma*, are the mental contents or factors of consciousness making up the single states of mind.

7. Literally, "setting up mindfulness in front."

himself. "Calming the activity of the (breath-) body, I shall breathe in," thus he trains himself. "Calming the activity of the (breath-) body, I shall breathe out," thus he trains himself.

Just as a skillful turner or turner's apprentice, making a long turn, knows, "I am making a long turn," or making a short turn, knows, "I am making a short turn," just so the monk, breathing in a long breath, knows, "I am breathing in a long breath"; breathing out a long breath, he knows, "I am breathing out a long breath"; breathing in a short breath, he knows, "I am breathing in a short breath"; breathing out a short breath, he knows, "I am breathing out a short breath." "Experiencing the whole (breath-) body, I shall breathe in," thus he trains himself. "Experiencing the whole (breath-) body, I shall breathe out," thus he trains himself. "Calming the activity of the (breath-) body, I shall breathe in," thus he trains himself. "Calming the activity of the (breath-) body, I shall breathe out," thus he trains himself.

Thus he lives contemplating the body in the body internally, or he lives contemplating the body in the body externally, or he lives contemplating the body in the body internally and externally.[8] He lives contemplating origination factors[9] in the body, or he lives contemplating

---

8. 'Internally': contemplating his own breathing; 'externally': contemplating another's breathing; 'internally and externally': contemplating one's own and another's breathing, alternately, with uninterrupted attention. In the beginning one pays attention to one's own breathing only, and it is only in advanced stages that for the sake of practicing insight, one by inference at times pays attention also to another person's process of breathing.

9. The origination factors *(samudaya-dhamma)*, that is, the conditions of the origination of the breath-body; these are: the body in its entirety, nasal aperture and mind.

dissolution factors[10] in the body, or he lives contemplating origination-and-dissolution factors[11] in the body. Or his mindfulness is established with the thought: "The body exists,"[12] to the extent necessary just for knowledge and mindfulness, and he lives detached,[13] and clings to nothing in the world. Thus also, monks, a monk lives contemplating the body in the body.

2. The Postures of the Body

And further, monks, a monk knows, when he is going, "I am going"; he knows, when he is standing, "I am standing"; he knows, when he is sitting, "I am sitting"; he knows, when he is lying down, "I am lying down"; or just as his body is disposed so he knows it.

Thus he lives contemplating the body in the body internally, or he lives contemplating the body in the body externally, or he lives contemplating the body in the body internally and externally. He lives contemplating origination factors in the body, or he lives contemplating dissolution factors in the body, or he lives contemplating origination-and-dissolution factors in the body.[14] Or his mindfulness is established with the thought: "The body exists," to the extent necessary just for knowledge and mindfulness, and he lives detached, and clings to nothing

---

10. The conditions of the dissolution of the breath-body are: the destruction of the body and of the nasal aperture, and the ceasing of mental activity.

11. The contemplation of both, alternately.

12. That is, only impersonal bodily processes exist, without a self, soul, spirit or abiding essence or substance. The corresponding phrase in the following contemplations should be understood accordingly.

13. Detached from craving and wrong view.

in the world. Thus also, monks, a monk lives contemplating the body in the body.

3. Mindfulness with Clear Comprehension

And further, monks, a monk, in going forward and back, applies clear comprehension; in looking straight on and looking away, he applies clear comprehension; in bending and in stretching, he applies clear comprehension; in wearing robes and carrying the bowl, he applies clear comprehension; in eating, drinking, chewing and savouring, he applies clear comprehension; in walking, in standing, in sitting, in falling asleep, in waking, in speaking and in keeping silence, he applies clear comprehension.

Thus he lives contemplating the body in the body…

4. The Reflection on the Repulsiveness of the Body

And further, monks, a monk reflects on this very body enveloped by the skin and full of manifold impurity, from the soles up, and from the top of the head-hairs down, thinking thus: "There are in this body hair of the head, hair of the body, nails, teeth, skin, flesh, sinews, bones, marrow, kidney, heart, liver, midriff, spleen, lungs, intestines, mesentery, gorge, faeces, bile, phlegm, pus, blood, sweat, fat, tears, grease, saliva, nasal mucus, synovial fluid, urine."

Just as if there were a double-mouthed provision bag full of various kinds of grain such as hill paddy, paddy, green gram, cow-peas, sesamum, and husked rice, and a

---

14. All contemplations of the body, excepting the preceding one, have as factors of origination: ignorance, craving, kamma, food, and the general characteristic of originating; the factors of dissolution are: disappearance of ignorance, craving, kamma, food, and the general characteristic of dissolving.

man with sound eyes, having opened that bag, were to take stock of the contents thus: "This is hill paddy, this is paddy, this is green gram, this is cow-pea, this is sesamum, this is husked rice." Just so, monks, a monk reflects on this very body enveloped by the skin and full of manifold impurity, from the soles up, and from the top of the head-hairs down, thinking thus: "There are in this body hair of the head, hair of the body, nails, teeth, skin, flesh, sinews, bones, marrow, kidney, heart, liver, midriff, spleen, lungs, intestines, mesentery, gorge, faeces, bile, phlegm, pus, blood, sweat, fat, tears, grease, saliva, nasal mucus, synovial fluid, urine."

Thus he lives contemplating the body in the body…

5. The Reflection on the Material Elements

And further, monks, a monk reflects on this very body, however it be placed or disposed, by way of the material elements: "There are in this body the element of earth, the element of water, the element of fire, the element of wind."[15]

Just as if, monks, a clever cow-butcher or his apprentice, having slaughtered a cow and divided it into portions, should be sitting at the junction of four high roads, in the same way, a monk reflects on this very body, as it is placed or disposed, by way of the material elements: "There are in this body the elements of earth, water, fire, and wind."

Thus he lives contemplating the body in the body…

---

15. The so-called 'elements' are the primary qualities of matter, explained by Buddhist tradition as solidity (earth), adhesion (water), caloricity (fire) and motion (wind or air).

6. The Nine Cemetery Contemplations

(1) And further, monks, as if a monk sees a body dead one, two, or three days; swollen, blue and festering, thrown in the charnel ground, he then applies this perception to his own body thus: "Verily, also my own body is of the same nature; such it will become and will not escape it."

> Thus he lives contemplating the body in the body internally, or he lives contemplating the body in the body externally, or he lives contemplating the body in the body internally and externally. He lives contemplating origination-factors in the body, or he lives contemplating dissolution factors in the body, or he lives contemplating origination-and-dissolution-factors in the body. Or his mindfulness is established with the thought: "The body exists," to the extent necessary just for knowledge and mindfulness, and he lives detached, and clings to nothing in the world. Thus also, monks, a monk lives contemplating the body in the body.

(2) And further, monks, as if a monk sees a body thrown in the charnel ground, being eaten by crows, hawks, vultures, dogs, jackals or by different kinds of worms, he then applies this perception to his own body thus: "Verily, also my own body is of the same nature; such it will become and will not escape it." Thus he lives contemplating the body in the body…

(3) And further, monks, as if a monk sees a body thrown in the charnel ground and reduced to a skeleton with some flesh and blood attached to it, held together by the tendons…

(4) And further, monks, as if a monk sees a body thrown in the charnel ground and reduced to a skeleton blood-besmeared and without flesh, held together by the tendons…

(5) And further, monks, as if a monk sees a body thrown in the charnel ground and reduced to a skeleton without flesh and blood, held together by the tendons…

(6) And further, monks, as if a monk sees a body thrown in the charnel ground and reduced to disconnected bones, scattered in all directions—here a bone of the hand, there a bone of the foot, a shin bone, a thigh bone, the pelvis, spine and skull…

(7) And further, monks, as if a monk sees a body thrown in the charnel ground, reduced to bleached bones of conchlike colour…

(8) And further, monks, as if a monk sees a body thrown in the charnel ground reduced to bones, more than a year-old, lying in a heap…

(9) And further, monks, as if a monk sees a body thrown in the charnel ground, reduced to bones gone rotten and become dust, he then applies this perception to his own body thus: "Verily, also my own body is of the same nature; such it will become and will not escape it."

Thus he lives contemplating the body in the body internally, or he lives contemplating the body in the body externally, or he lives contemplating the body in the body internally and externally. He lives contemplating origination factors in the body, or he lives contemplating dissolution factors in the body, or he lives contemplating origination-and-dissolution factors in the body. Or his mindfulness is established with the thought: "The body exists," to the extent necessary just for knowledge and mindfulness, and he lives detached, and clings to nothing in the world. Thus also, monks, a monk lives contemplating the body in the body.

II. THE CONTEMPLATION OF FEELING

And how, monks, does a monk live contemplating feelings in feelings?

Herein, monks, a monk when experiencing a pleasant feeling knows, "I experience a pleasant feeling"; when experiencing a painful feeling, he knows, "I experience a painful feeling"; when experiencing a neither-pleasant-nor-painful feeling," he knows, "I experience a neither-pleasant-nor-painful feeling." When experiencing a pleasant worldly feeling, he knows, "I experience a pleasant worldly feeling"; when experiencing a pleasant spiritual feeling, he knows, "I experience a pleasant spiritual feeling"; when experiencing a painful worldly feeling, he knows, "I experience a painful worldly feeling"; when experiencing a painful spiritual feeling, he knows, "I experience a painful spiritual feeling"; when experiencing a neither-pleasant-nor-painful worldly feeling, he knows, "I experience a neither-pleasant-nor-painful worldly feeling"; when experiencing a neither-pleasant-nor-painful spiritual feeling, he knows, "I experience a neither-pleasant-nor-painful spiritual feeling."

Thus he lives contemplating feelings in feelings internally, or he lives contemplating feelings in feelings externally, or he lives contemplating feelings in feelings internally and externally. He lives contemplating origination factors in feelings, or he lives contemplating dissolution factors in feelings, or he lives contemplating origination-and-dissolution factors in feelings.[16] Or his mindfulness is established with the thought, "Feeling

---

16. The factors of origination are here: ignorance, craving, kamma, and sense-impression, and the general characteristic of originating; the factors of dissolution are: the disappearance of the four, and the general characteristic of dissolving.

exists," to the extent necessary just for knowledge and mindfulness, and he lives detached, and clings to nothing in the world. Thus, monks, a monk lives contemplating feelings in feelings.

III. THE CONTEMPLATION OF CONSCIOUSNESS

And how, monks, does a monk live contemplating consciousness in consciousness?

Herein, monks, a monk knows the consciousness with lust, as with lust; the consciousness without lust, as without lust; the consciousness with hate, as with hate; the consciousness without hate, as without hate; the consciousness with ignorance, as with ignorance; the consciousness without ignorance, as without ignorance; the shrunken state of consciousness, as the shrunken state;[17] the distracted state of consciousness, as the distracted state;[18] the developed state of consciousness as the developed state;[19] the undeveloped state of consciousness as the undeveloped state;[20] the state of consciousness with some other mental state superior to it, as the state with something mentally higher;[21] the state of consciousness with no other mental state superior to it, as the state with nothing mentally higher;[22] the concentrated state of con-

---

17. This refers to a rigid and indolent state of mind.
18. This refers to a restless mind.
19. The consciousness of the meditative absorptions of the fine-corporeal and uncorporeal sphere *(rūpa-arūpa-jhāna)*.
20. The ordinary consciousness of the sensuous state of existence *(kāmāvacara)*.
21. The consciousness of the sensuous state of existence, having other mental states superior to it.
22. The consciousness of the fine-corporeal and the uncorporeal spheres, having no mundane mental state superior to it.

sciousness, as the concentrated state; the unconcentrated state of consciousness, as the unconcentrated state; the freed state of consciousness, as the freed state;[23] and the unfreed state of consciousness as the unfreed state.

Thus he lives contemplating consciousness in consciousness internally, or he lives contemplating consciousness in consciousness externally, or he lives contemplating consciousness in consciousness internally and externally. He lives contemplating origination factors in consciousness, or he lives contemplating dissolution-factors in consciousness, or he lives contemplating origination-and-dissolution factors in consciousness.[24] Or his mindfulness is established with the thought, "Consciousness exists," to the extent necessary just for knowledge and mindfulness, and he lives detached, and clings to nothing in the world. Thus, monks, a monk lives contemplating consciousness in consciousness.

IV. THE CONTEMPLATION OF MENTAL OBJECTS
1. The Five Hindrances

And how, monks, does a monk live contemplating mental objects in mental objects?

Herein, monks, a monk lives contemplating mental objects in the mental objects of the five hindrances.

---

23. Temporarily freed from the defilements either through the methodical practice of insight *(vipassanā)* freeing from single evil states by force of their opposites, or through the meditative absorptions *(jhāna)*.

24. The factors of origination consist here of ignorance, craving, kamma, body-and-mind *(nāma-rūpa)*, and the general characteristic of originating; the factors of dissolution are: the disappearance of ignorance, etc., and the general characteristic of dissolving.

How, monks, does a monk live contemplating mental objects in the mental objects of the five hindrances?

Herein, monks, when *sense-desire* is present, a monk knows, "There is sense-desire in me," or when sense-desire is not present, he knows, "There is no sense-desire in me." He knows how the arising of the non-arisen sense-desire comes to be; he knows how the abandoning of the arisen sense-desire comes to be; and he knows how the non-arising in the future of the abandoned sense-desire comes to be.

When *anger* is present, he knows, "There is anger in me," or when anger is not present, he knows, "There is no anger in me." He knows how the arising of the non-arisen anger comes to be; he knows how the abandoning of the arisen anger comes to be; and he knows how the non-arising in the future of the abandoned anger comes to be.

When *sloth and torpor* are present, he knows, "There are sloth and torpor in me," or when sloth and torpor are not present, he knows, "There are no sloth and torpor in me." He knows how the arising of the non-arisen sloth and torpor comes to be; he knows how the abandoning of the arisen sloth and torpor comes to be; and he knows how the non-arising in the future of the abandoned sloth and torpor comes to be.

When *agitation and remorse* are present, he knows, "There are agitation and remorse in me," or when agitation and remorse are not present, he knows, "There are no agitation and remorse in me." He knows how the arising of the non-arisen agitation and remorse comes to be; he knows how the abandoning of the arisen agitation and remorse comes to be; and he knows how the non-arising in the future of the abandoned agitation and remorse comes to be.

When *doubt* is present, he knows, "There is doubt in me," or when doubt is not present, he knows, "There is no doubt in me." He knows how the arising of the non-arisen doubt comes to be; he knows how the abandoning of the arisen doubt comes to be; and he knows how the non-arising in the future of the abandoned doubt comes to be.

Thus he lives contemplating mental objects in mental objects internally, or he lives contemplating mental objects in mental objects externally, or he lives contemplating mental objects in mental objects internally and externally. He lives contemplating origination factors in mental objects, or he lives contemplating dissolution factors in mental objects, or he lives contemplating origination-and-dissolution factors in mental objects.[25] Or his mindfulness is established with the thought, "Mental objects exist," to the extent necessary just for knowledge and mindfulness, and he lives detached, and clings to nothing in the world. Thus also, monks, a monk lives contemplating mental objects in the mental objects of the five hindrances.

2. The Five Aggregates of Clinging

And further, monks, a monk lives contemplating mental objects in the mental objects of the five aggregates of clinging.[26]

How, monks, does a monk live contemplating mental objects in the mental objects of the five aggregates of clinging?

Herein, monks, a monk thinks, "Thus is *material form;*

---

25. The factors of origination are here the conditions which produce the hindrances, such as wrong reflection, etc., the factors of dissolution are the conditions which remove the hindrances, e.g., right reflection.

26. These five groups or aggregates constitute the so-called personality. By making them objects of clinging, existence, in the form of repeated births and deaths, is perpetuated.

thus is the arising of material form; and thus is the disappearance of material form. Thus is *feeling;* thus is the arising of feeling; and thus is the disappearance of feeling. Thus is *perception;* thus is the arising of perception; and thus is the disappearance of perception. Thus are *formations;* thus is the arising of formations; and thus is the disappearance of formations. Thus is *consciousness;* thus is the arising of consciousness; and thus is the disappearance of consciousness."

Thus he lives contemplating mental objects in mental objects internally, or he lives contemplating mental objects in mental objects externally, or he lives contemplating mental objects in mental objects internally and externally. He lives contemplating origination factors in mental objects, or he lives contemplating dissolution factors in mental objects, or he lives contemplating origination-and-dissolution factors in mental objects.[27] Or his mindfulness is established with the thought, "Mental objects exist," to the extent necessary just for knowledge and mindfulness, and he lives detached, and clings to nothing in the world. Thus also, monks, a monk lives contemplating mental objects in the mental objects of the five aggregates of clinging.

---

27. The origination-and-dissolution factors of the five aggregates: for material form, the same as for the postures (Note 10); for feeling, the same as for the contemplation of feeling (Note 12); for perception and formations, the same as for feeling (Note 12); for consciousness, the same as for the contemplation of consciousness (Note 20).

3. The Six Internal and External Sense Bases

And further, monks, a monk lives contemplating mental objects in the mental objects of the six internal and the six external sense-bases.

How, monks, does a monk live contemplating mental objects in the mental objects of the six internal and the six external sense-bases?

Herein, monks, a monk knows the eye and visual forms and the fetter that arises dependent on both (the eye and forms);[28] he knows how the arising of the non-arisen fetter comes to be; he knows how the abandoning of the arisen fetter comes to be; and he knows how the non-arising in the future of the abandoned fetter comes to be.

He knows the *ear* and *sounds* … the *nose* and *smells* … the *tongue* and *flavours* … the *body* and *tactual objects* … the *mind* and *mental objects,* and the fetter that arises dependent on both; he knows how the arising of the non-arisen fetter comes to be; he knows how the abandoning of the arisen fetter comes to be; and he knows how the non-arising in the future of the abandoned fetter comes to be.

Thus he lives contemplating mental objects in mental objects internally, or he lives contemplating mental objects in mental objects externally, or he lives contemplating mental objects in mental objects internally and externally. He lives contemplating origination factors in mental objects, or he lives contemplating dissolution factors in mental objects, or he lives contemplating origination-and-

---

28. The usual enumeration of the ten principal fetters *(saṃyojana),* as given in the Discourse Collection (Sutta Piṭaka), is as follows: (1) self-illusion, (2) scepticism, (3) attachment to rules and rituals, (4) sensual lust, (5) ill-will, (6) craving for fine-corporeal existence, (7) craving for incorporeal existence, (8) conceit, (9) restlessness, (10) ignorance.

dissolution factors in mental objects.[29] Or his mindfulness is established with the thought, "Mental objects exist," to the extent necessary just for knowledge and mindfulness, and he lives detached, and clings to nothing in the world. Thus, monks, a monk lives contemplating mental objects in the mental objects of the six internal and the six external sense-bases.

4. The Seven Factors of Enlightenment

And further, monks, a monk lives contemplating mental objects in the mental objects of the seven factors of enlightenment.

How, monks, does a monk live contemplating mental objects in the mental objects of the seven factors of enlightenment?

Herein, monks, when the enlightenment-factor of *mindfulness* is present, the monk knows, "The enlightenment-factor of mindfulness is in me," or when the enlightenment-factor of mindfulness is absent, he knows, "The enlightenment-factor of mindfulness is not in me"; and he knows how the arising of the non-arisen enlightenment-factor of mindfulness comes to be; and how perfection in the development of the arisen enlightenment-factor of mindfulness comes to be.

When the enlightenment-factor of *the investigation of mental objects* is present, the monk knows, "The enlightenment-factor of the investigation of mental objects

---

29. Origination factors of the ten physical sense-bases are ignorance, craving, kamma, food, and the general characteristic of originating; dissolution factors: the general characteristic of dissolving and the disappearance of ignorance, etc. The origination-and-dissolution factors of the mind-base are the same as those of feeling (Note 12).

is in me"; when the enlightenment-factor of the investigation of mental objects is absent, he knows, "The enlightenment-factor of the investigation of mental objects is not in me"; and he knows how the arising of the non-arisen enlightenment-factor of the investigation of mental objects comes to be, and how perfection in the development of the arisen enlightenment-factor of the investigation of mental objects comes to be.

When the enlightenment-factor of *energy* is present, he knows, "The enlightenment-factor of energy is in me"; when the enlightenment-factor of energy is absent, he knows, "The enlightenment-factor of energy is not in me"; and he knows how the arising of the non-arisen enlightenment-factor of energy comes to be, and how perfection in the development of the arisen enlightenment-factor of energy comes to be.

When the enlightenment-factor of *joy* is present, he knows, "The enlightenment-factor of joy is in me"; when the enlightenment-factor of joy is absent, he knows, "The enlightenment-factor of joy is not in me"; and he knows how the arising of the non-arisen enlightenment-factor of joy comes to be, and how perfection in the development of the arisen enlightenment-factor of joy comes to be.

When the enlightenment-factor of *tranquillity* is present, he knows, "The enlightenment-factor of tranquillity is in me"; when the enlightenment-factor of tranquillity is absent, he knows, "The enlightenment-factor of tranquillity is not in me"; and he knows how the arising of the non-arisen enlightenment-factor of tranquillity comes to be, and how perfection in the development of the arisen enlightenment-factor of tranquillity comes to be.

When the enlightenment-factor of *concentration* is present, he knows, "The enlightenment-factor of concentration is in me"; when the enlightenment-factor of concentration is absent, he knows, "The enlightenment-factor of concentration is not in me"; and he knows how the arising of the non-arisen enlightenment-factor of concentration comes to be, and how perfection in the development of the arisen enlightenment-factor of concentration comes to be.

When the enlightenment-factor of *equanimity* is present, he knows, "The enlightenment-factor of equanimity is in me"; when the enlightenment-factor of equanimity is absent, he knows, "The enlightenment-factor of equanimity is not in me"; and he knows how the arising of the non-arisen enlightenment-factor of equanimity comes to be, and how perfection in the development of the arisen enlightenment-factor of equanimity comes to be.

Thus he lives contemplating mental objects in mental objects internally, or he lives contemplating mental objects in mental objects externally, or he lives contemplating mental objects in mental objects internally and externally. He lives contemplating origination-factors in mental objects, or he lives contemplating dissolution-factors in mental objects, or he lives contemplating origination-and-dissolution-factors in mental objects.[30] Or his mindfulness is established with the thought, "Mental objects exist," to the extent necessary just for knowledge and mindfulness, and he lives detached, and clings to nothing in the world. Thus, monks, a monk lives contemplating mental objects in the mental objects of the seven factors of enlightenment.

---

30. Just the conditions conducive to the origination and dissolution of the factors of enlightenment comprise the origination-and-dissolution factors here.

5. The Four Noble Truths

And further, monks, a monk lives contemplating mental objects in the mental objects of the four noble truths.

How, monks, does a monk live contemplating mental objects in the mental objects of the four noble truths?

Herein, monks, a monk knows, "This is suffering," according to reality; he knows, "This is the origin of suffering," according to reality; he knows, "This is the cessation of suffering," according to reality; he knows "This is the road leading to the cessation of suffering," according to reality.

Thus he lives contemplating mental objects in mental objects internally, or he lives contemplating mental objects in mental objects externally, or he lives contemplating mental objects in mental objects internally and externally. He lives contemplating origination-factors in mental objects, or he lives contemplating dissolution-factors in mental objects, or he lives contemplating origination-and-dissolution-factors in mental objects.[31] Or his mindfulness is established with the thought, "Mental objects exist," to the extent necessary just for knowledge and mindfulness, and he lives detached, and clings to nothing in the world. Thus, monks, a monk lives contemplating mental objects in the mental objects of the four noble truths.

Verily, monks, whosoever practices these four foundations of mindfulness in this manner for seven years, then one of these two fruits may be expected by him: highest knowledge (arahantship) here and now, or if some remainder of clinging is yet present, the state of

---

31. The origination-and-dissolution factors of the truths should be understood as the arising and passing of suffering, craving, and the path; the truth of cessation is not to be included in this contemplation since it has neither origination nor dissolution.

nonreturning.[32]

O monks, let alone seven years. Should any person practice these four foundations of mindfulness in this manner for six years… five years… four years… three years… two years… one year, then one of these two fruits may be expected by him: highest knowledge here and now, or if some remainder of clinging is yet present, the state of nonreturning.

O monks, let alone a year. Should any person practice these four foundations of mindfulness in this manner for seven months… six months… five months… four months… three months… two months… a month… half a month, then one of these two fruits may be expected by him: highest knowledge here and now, or if some remainder of clinging is yet present, the state of nonreturning.

O monks, let alone half a month. Should any person practice these four foundations of mindfulness in this manner for a week, then one of these two fruits may be expected by him: highest knowledge here and now, or if some remainder of clinging is yet present, the state of nonreturning.

Because of this it was said: "This is the only way, monks, for the purification of beings, for the overcoming of sorrow and lamentation, for the destruction of suffering and grief, for reaching the right path, for the attainment of Nibbāna, namely the four foundations of mindfulness."

Thus spoke the Blessed One. Satisfied, the monks approved of his words.

* * *

---

32. That is, the non-returning to the world of sensuality. This is the last stage before the attainment of the final goal of arahantship

THE BUDDHIST PUBLICATION SOCIETY

The BPS is an approved charity dedicated to making known the Teaching of the Buddha, which has a vital message for all people.

Founded in 1958, the BPS has published a wide variety of books and booklets covering a great range of topics. Its publications include accurate annotated translations of the Buddha's discourses, standard reference works, as well as original contemporary expositions of Buddhist thought and practice. These works present Buddhism as it truly is—a dynamic force which has influenced receptive minds for the past 2500 years and is still as relevant today as it was when it first arose.

You can support the BPS by becoming a member. All members receive the biannual membership book and are entitled to discounts on BPS books.

For more information about the BPS and our publications, please visit our website, or write an e-mail, or a letter to the:

Administrative Secretary
Buddhist Publication Society
P.O. Box 61
54 Sangharaja Mawatha
Kandy • Sri Lanka
E-mail: bps@bps.lk
web site: http://www.bps.lk
Tel: 0094 81 223 7283 • Fax: 0094 81 222 3679